Paper Textures

Royalty-free Art for Designers

Ginny Parfitt

Schiffer® Publishing Ltd
4880 Lower Valley Road, Atglen, PA 19310 USA

I0800667

Contents

NOTICE OF RIGHTS

These images are copyrighted pursuant to 17 U.S.C. 101 et seq. The purchase of this book and accompanying CD gives you a limited license to use up to five images on the CD for personal or commercial projects, without additional compensation or permission. Any other republication or reproduction of any image in this book or on this CD by any other graphic service, including print, electronic, known, and unknown sources, is strictly prohibited, as is the transmission of files.

Images on the CD are presented at approximately 4" x 6" at 300 dpi. Larger images are available from the publisher at appropriate rates. Use the link on the CD to the Schiffer Publishing website. All contact information can be found there.

Managing Editor: Ginny Parfitt
Cover and Book Design: John Cheek

Copyright © 2005 by Schiffer Publishing, Ltd.
Library of Congress Control Number: 2005921199

All rights reserved. No part of this work may be reproduced or used in any form or by any means—graphic, electronic, or mechanical, including photocopying or information storage and retrieval systems—without written permission from the publisher.

The scanning, uploading and distribution of this book or any part thereof via the Internet or via any other means without the permission of the publisher is illegal and punishable by law. Please purchase only authorized editions and do not participate in or encourage the electronic piracy of copyrighted materials.

"Schiffer," "Schiffer Publishing Ltd. & Design," and the "Design of pen and ink well" are registered trademarks of Schiffer Publishing Ltd.

Type set in Lydian BT/Korinna BT

ISBN: 0-7643-2118-8
Printed in China

Published by Schiffer Publishing Ltd.
4880 Lower Valley Road
Atglen, PA 19310
Phone: (610) 593-1777; Fax: (610) 593-2002
E-mail: Info@schifferbooks.com

For the largest selection of fine reference books on this and related subjects, please visit our web site at **www.schifferbooks.com**
We are always looking for people to write books on new and related subjects. If you have an idea for a book please contact us at the above address.

This book may be purchased from the publisher.
Include $3.95 for shipping.
Please try your bookstore first.
You may write for a free catalog.

In Europe, Schiffer books are distributed by
Bushwood Books
6 Marksbury Ave.
Kew Gardens
Surrey TW9 4JF England
Phone: 44 (0) 20 8392-8585;
Fax: 44 (0) 20 8392-9876
E-mail: info@bushwoodbooks.co.uk
Free postage in the U.K., Europe; air mail at cost.

Botanical

Botanical

Effect: Hue/Saturation

Effect: Hue/Saturation

Effect: Hue/Saturation

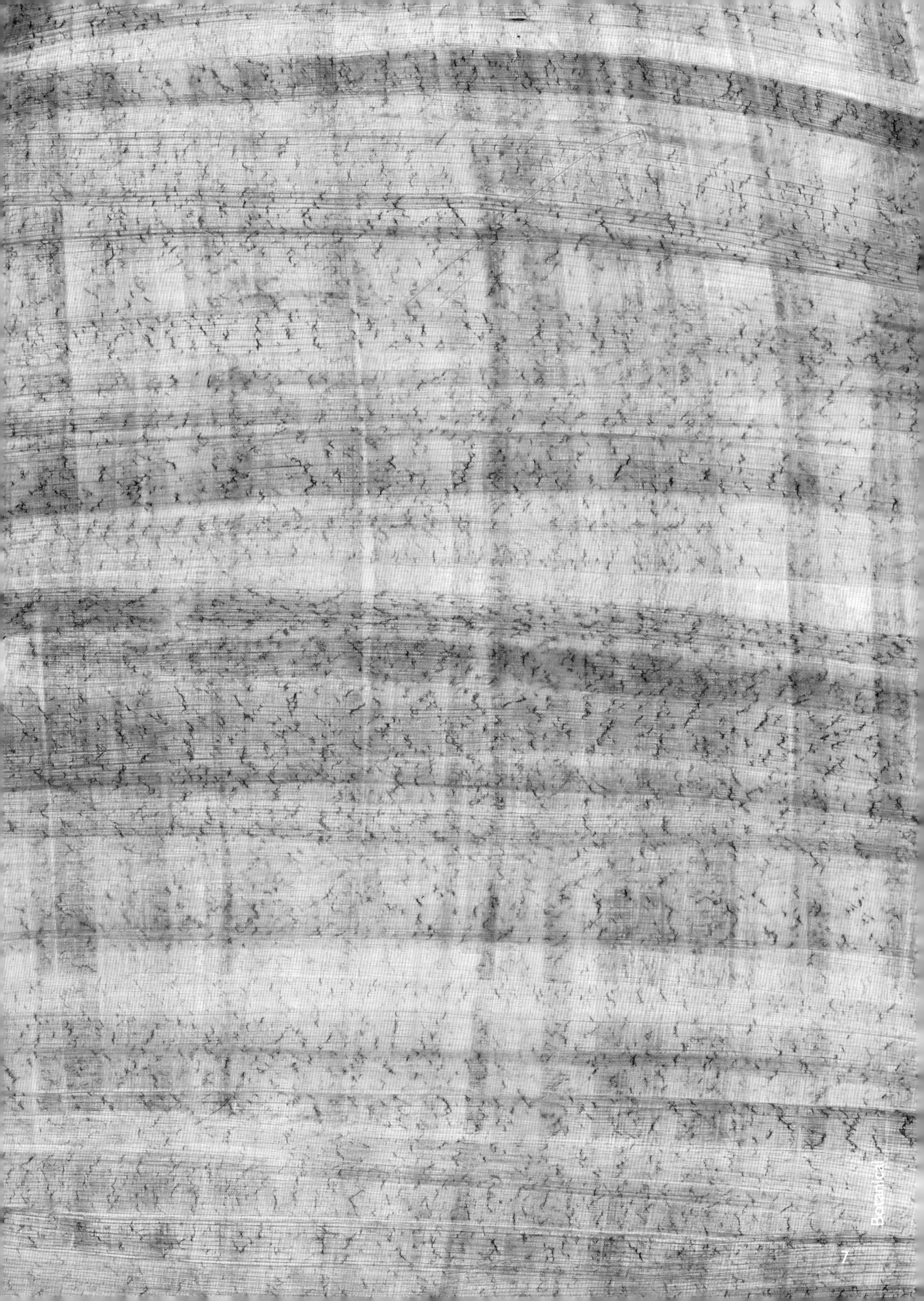

Botanical

Botanical

Light

Light

Filter: Extrude

Filter: Film Grain

Filter: Glowing Edges

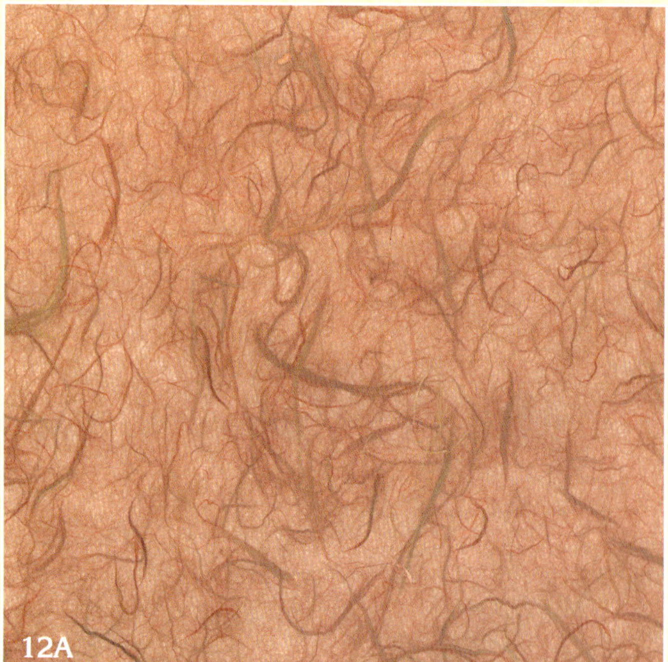
12A

Light

Bright

15A

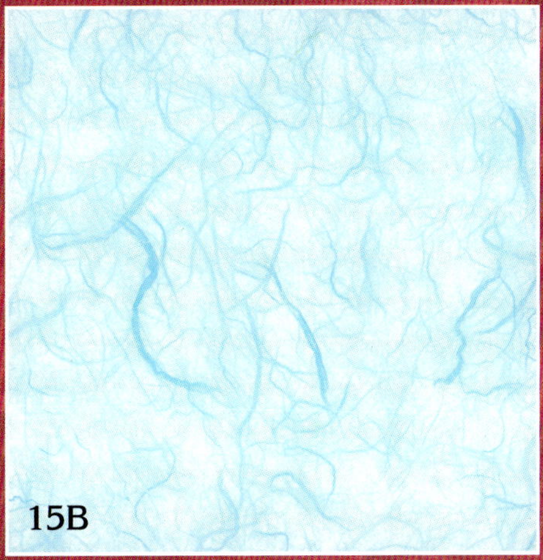

15B

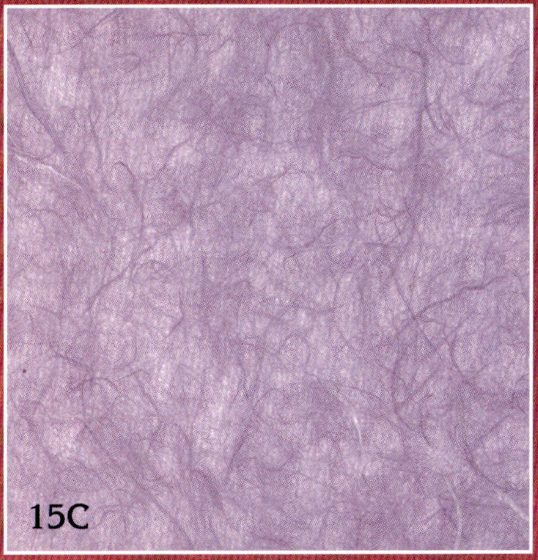

15C

17A

17B

Light

Neutral

Filter: Emboss

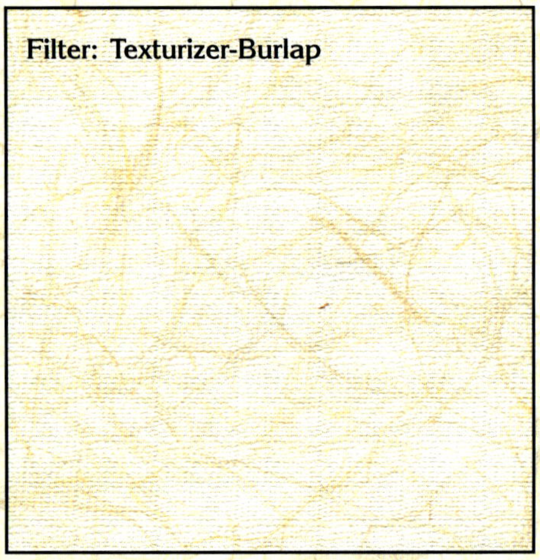

Filter: Texturizer-Burlap

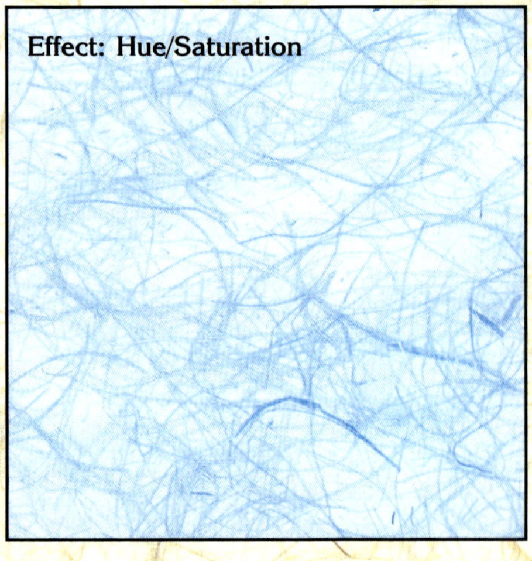

Effect: Hue/Saturation

Neutral

Neutral

Neutral

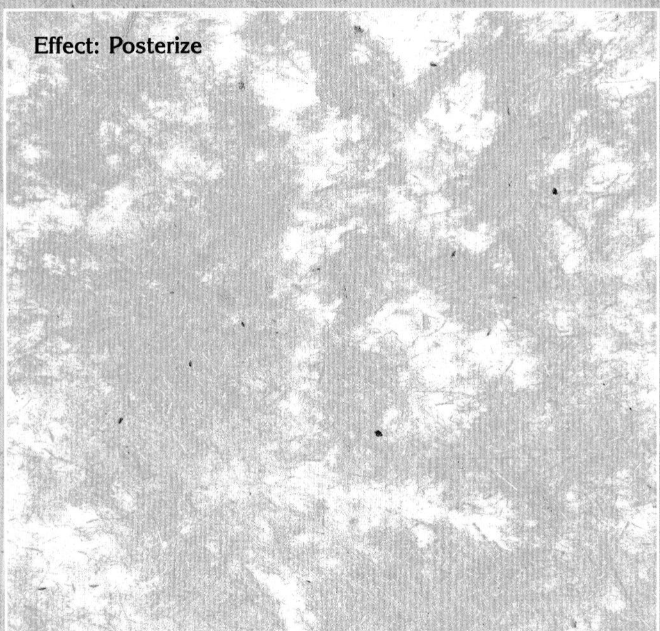

Effect: Posterize

Neutral

Neutral

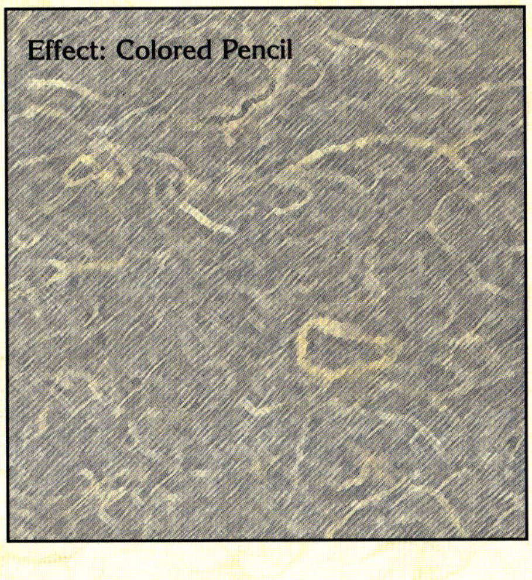
Effect: Colored Pencil

Effect: Neon Glow

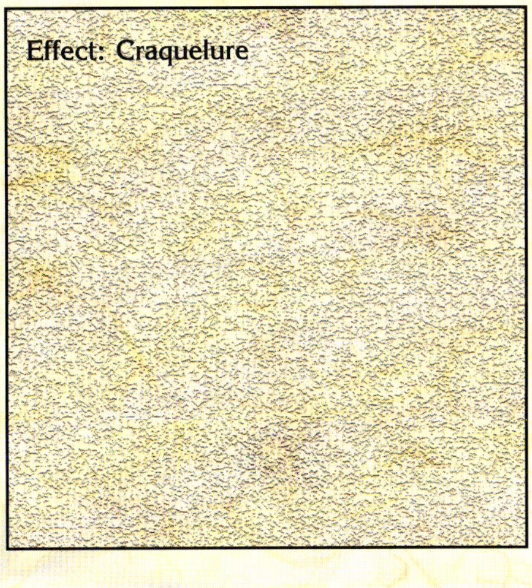
Effect: Craquelure

Neutral

Dark

Dark

Dark

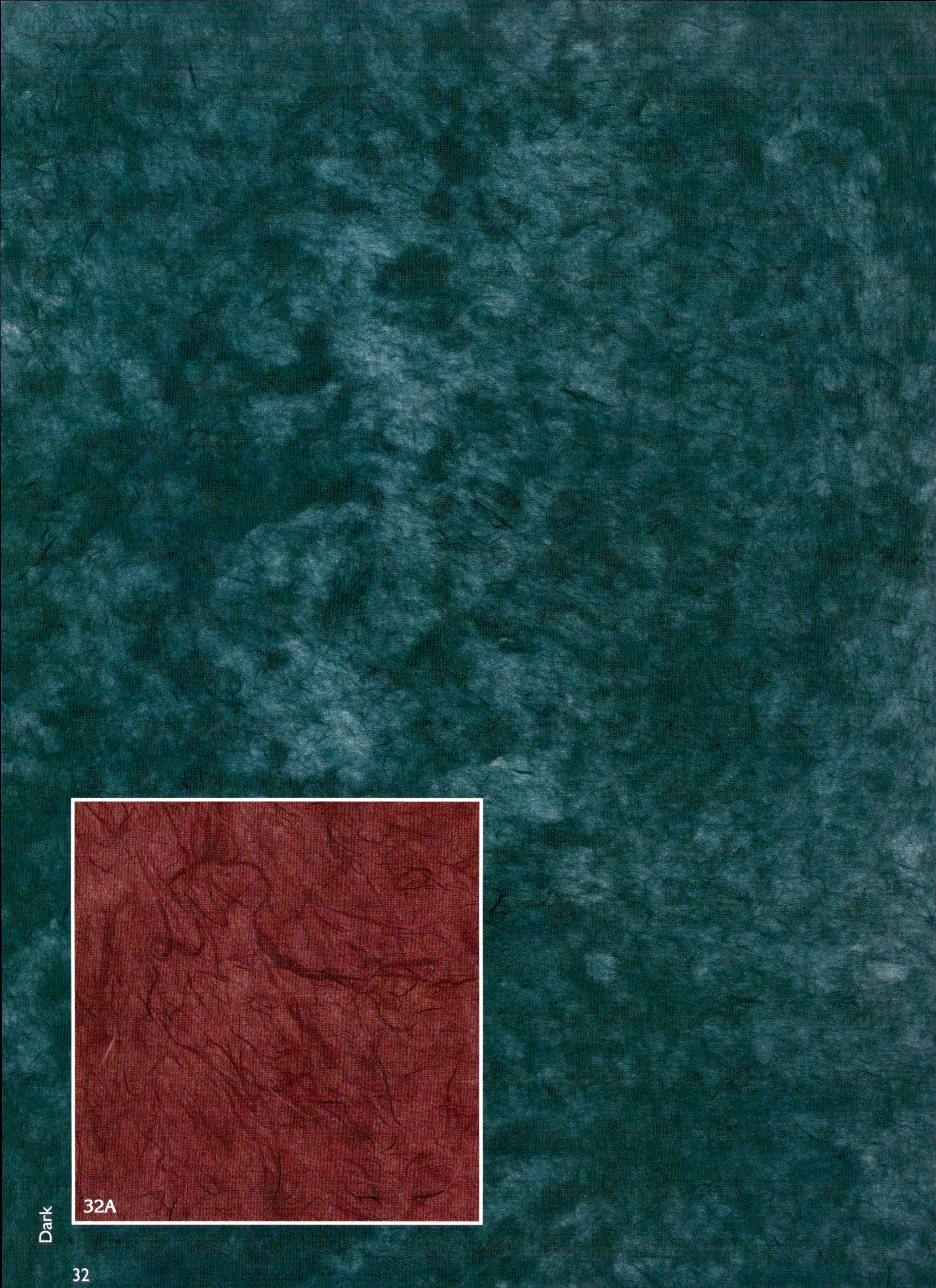

32A

33A

Dark

Dark

Marbled

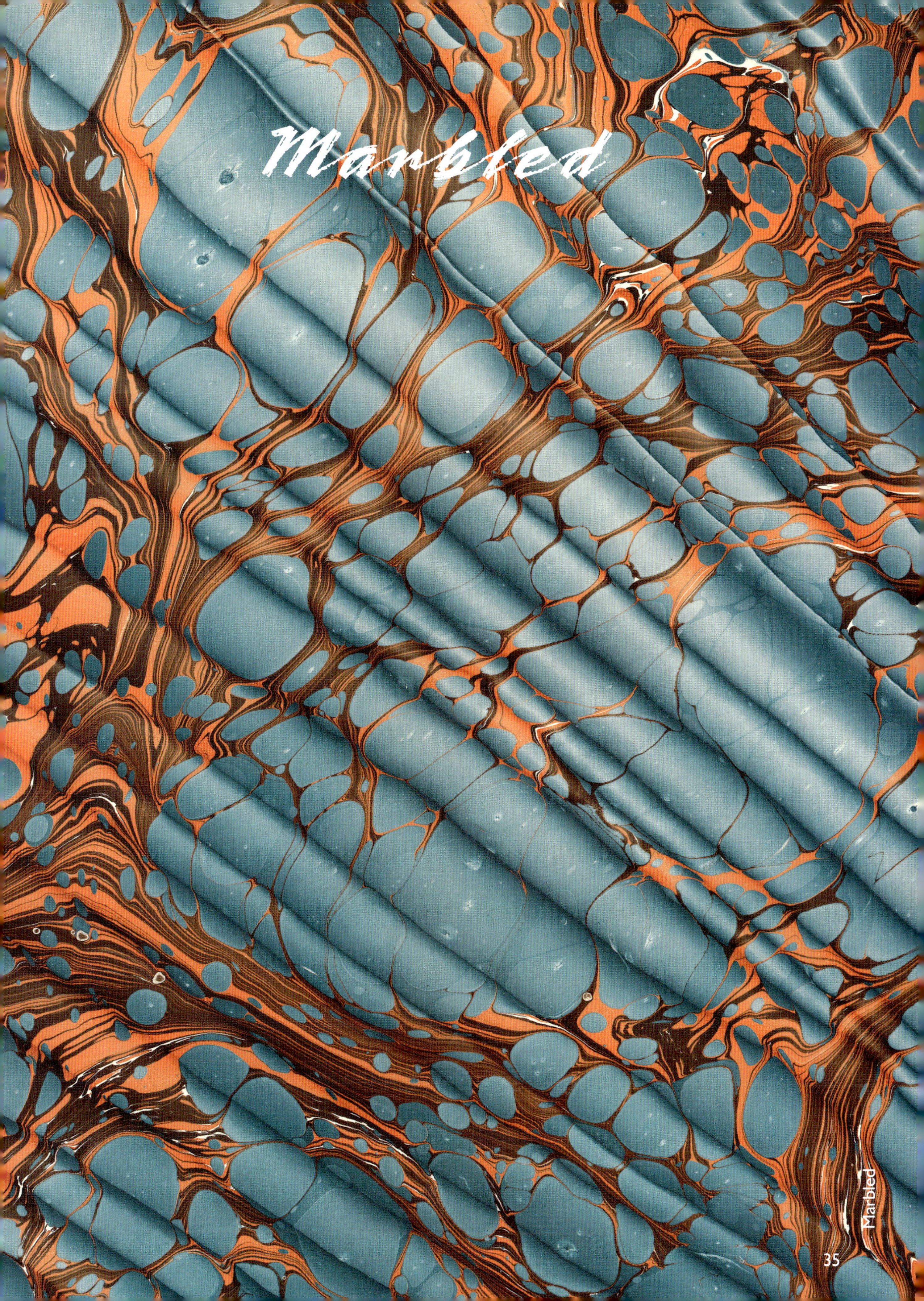

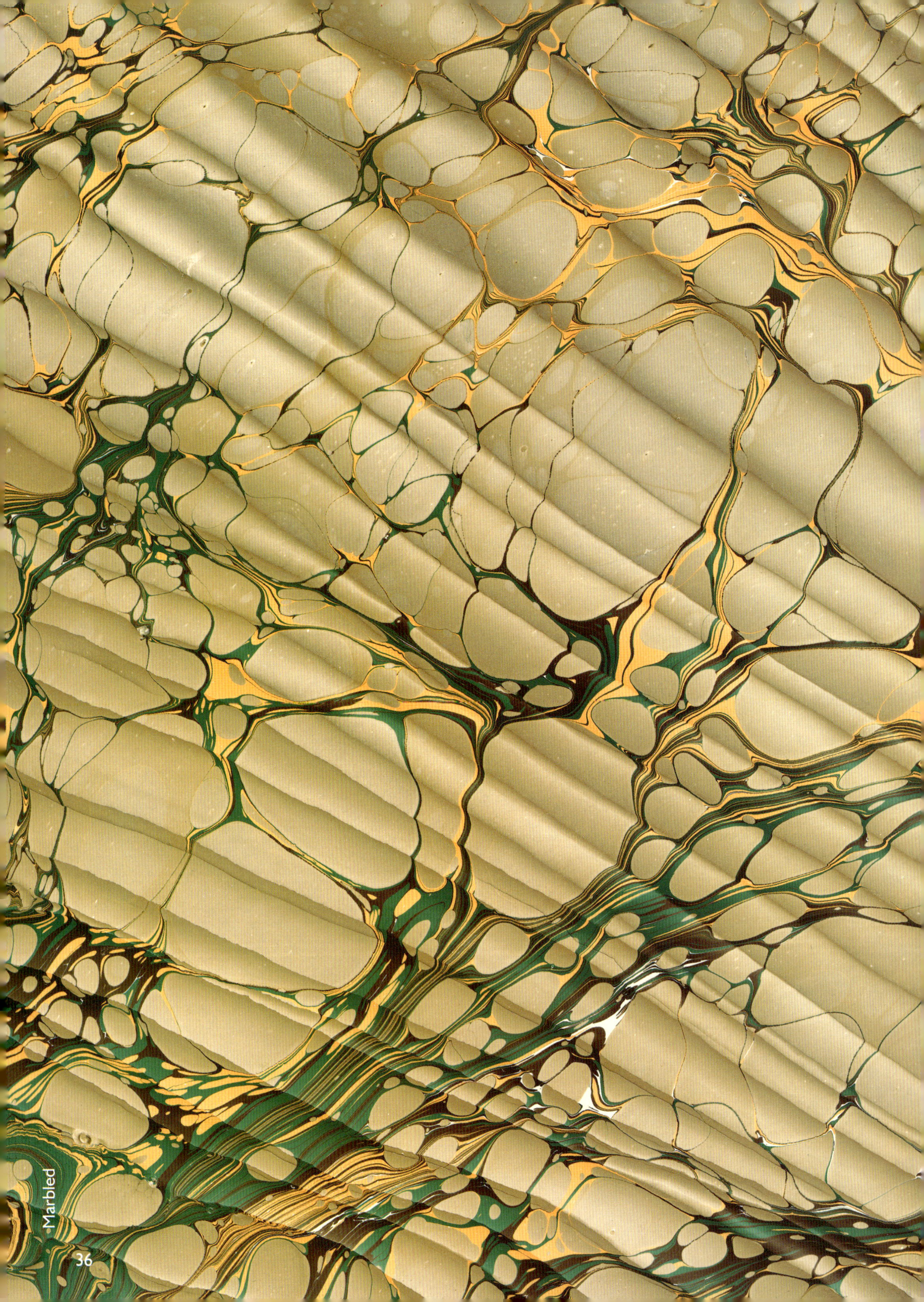

Marbled

Marbled

Marbled

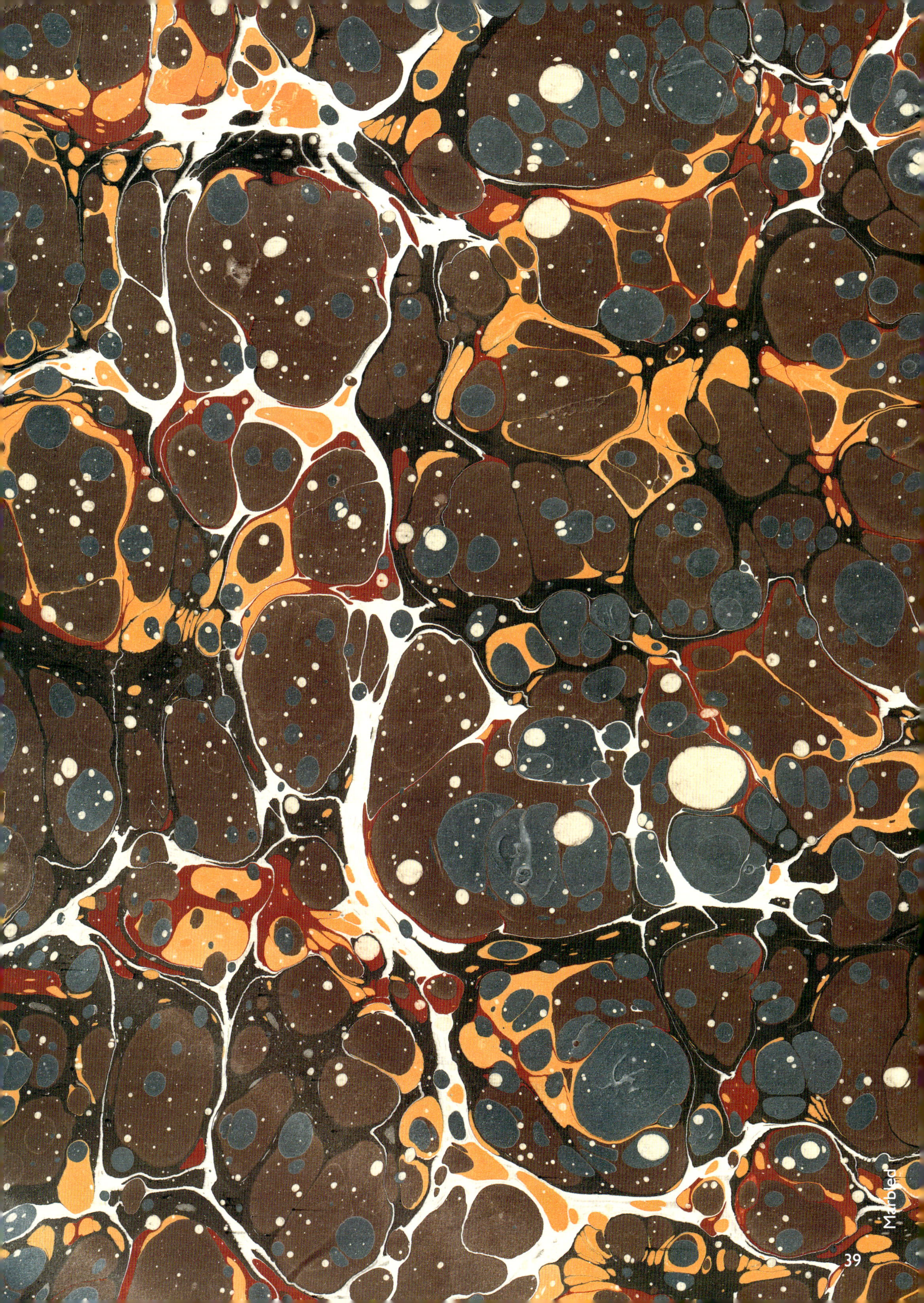
Marbled

Marbled

Filter: Twirl
Effect: Hue/Saturation

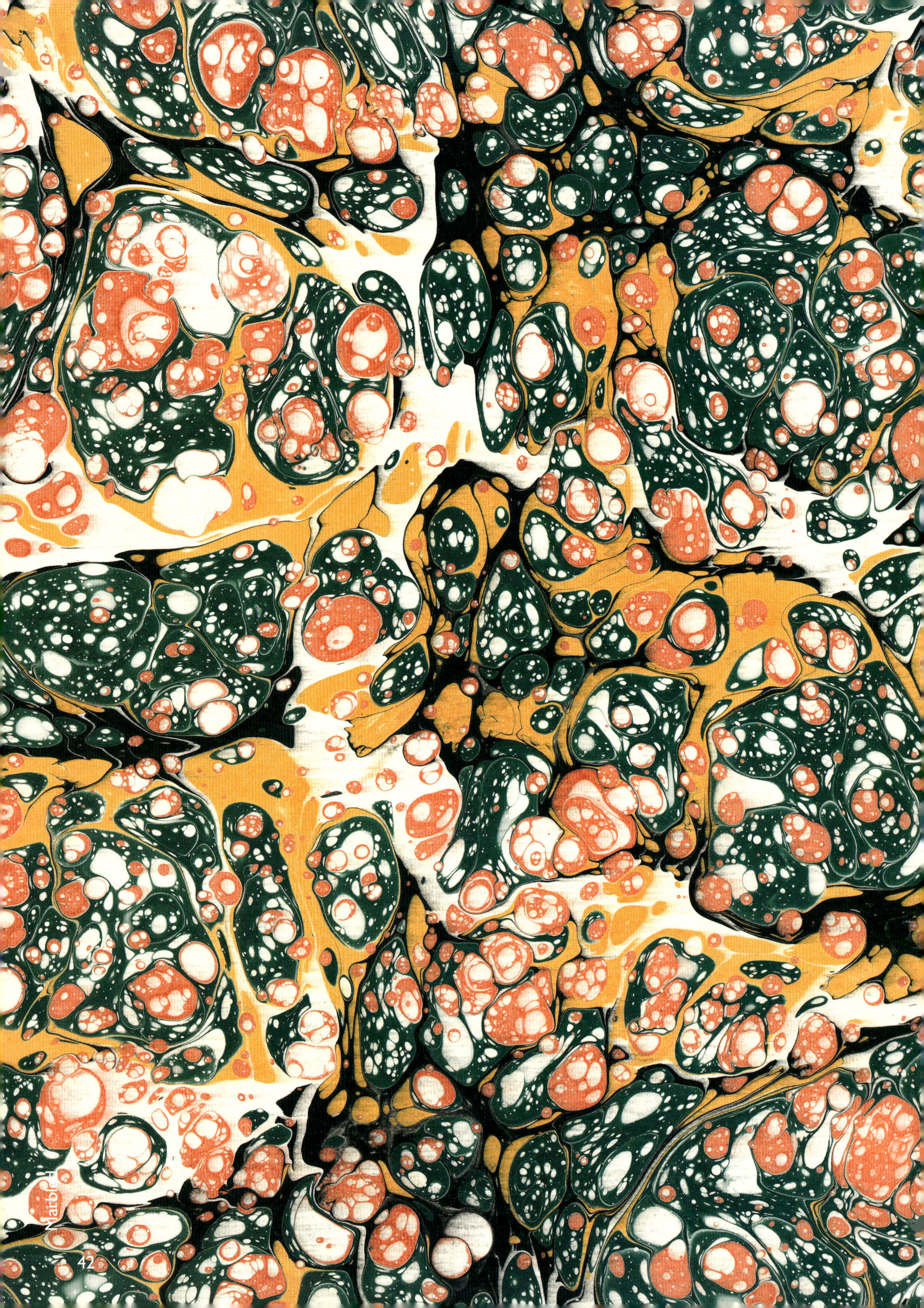

Filter: Tiles

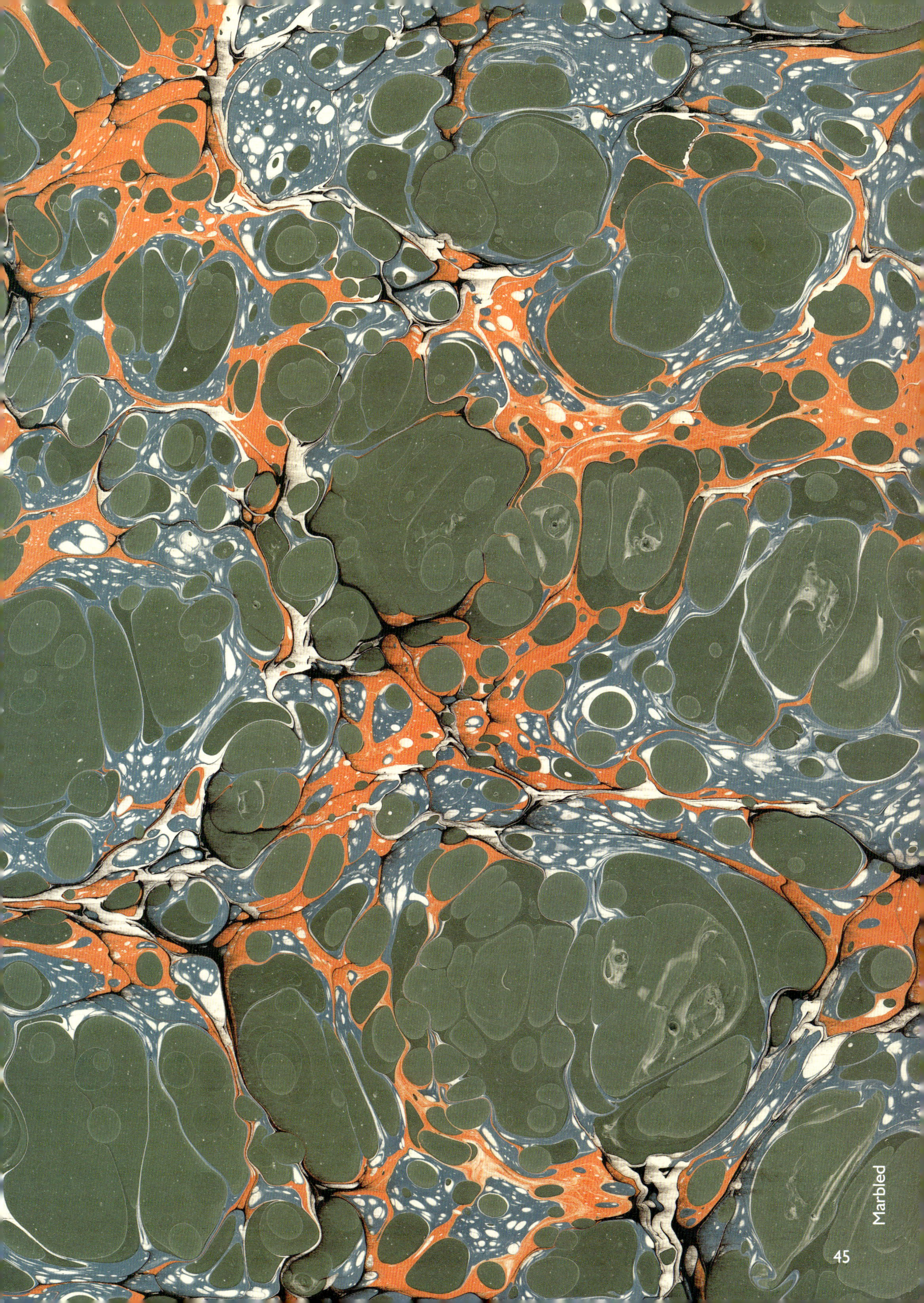

Marbled

Effects: Grayscale, Brightness/Contrast
Filter: Ripple

Marbled

Marbled

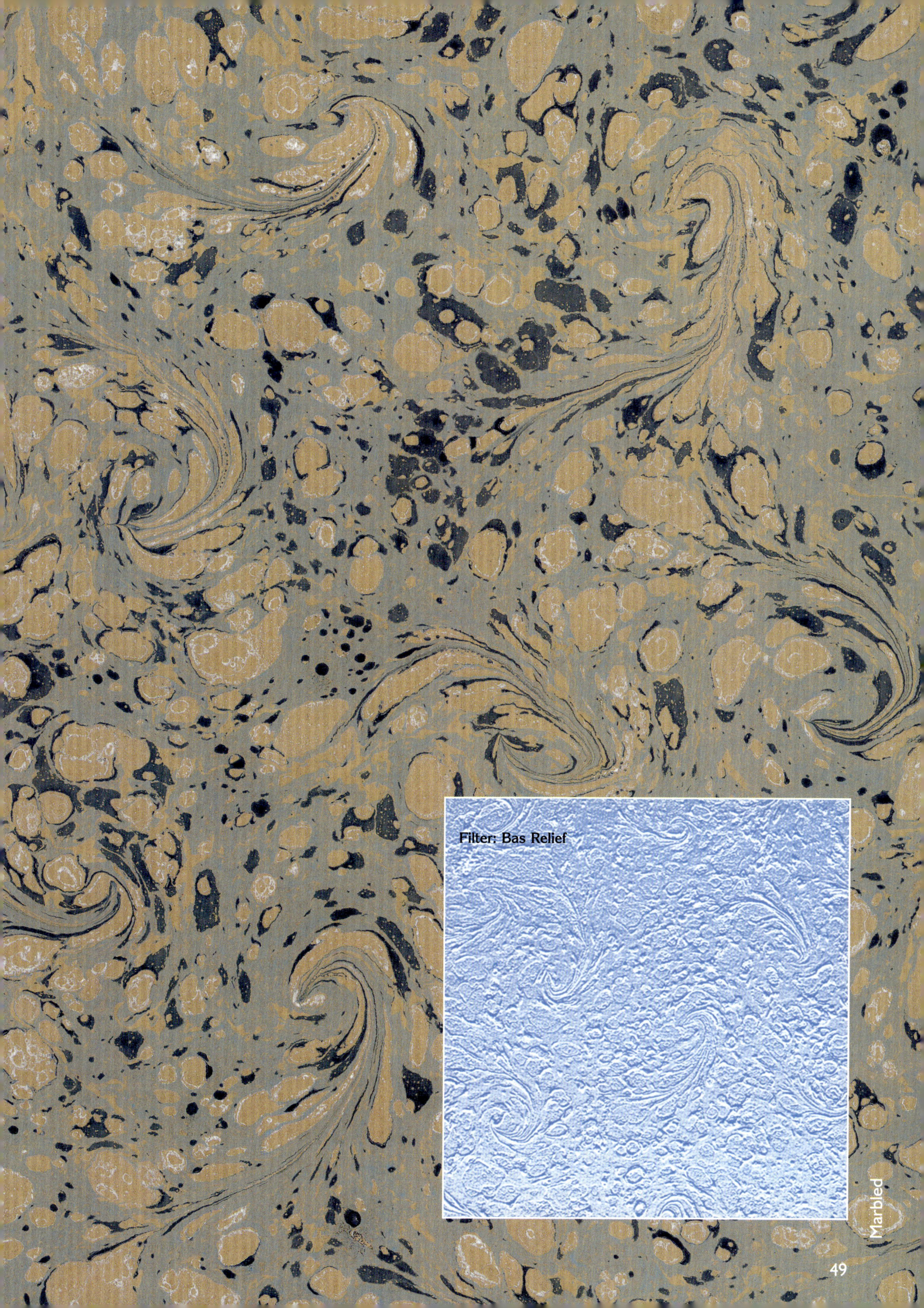

Filter: Bas Relief

Marbled

Marbled

Filter: Texturizer-Brick

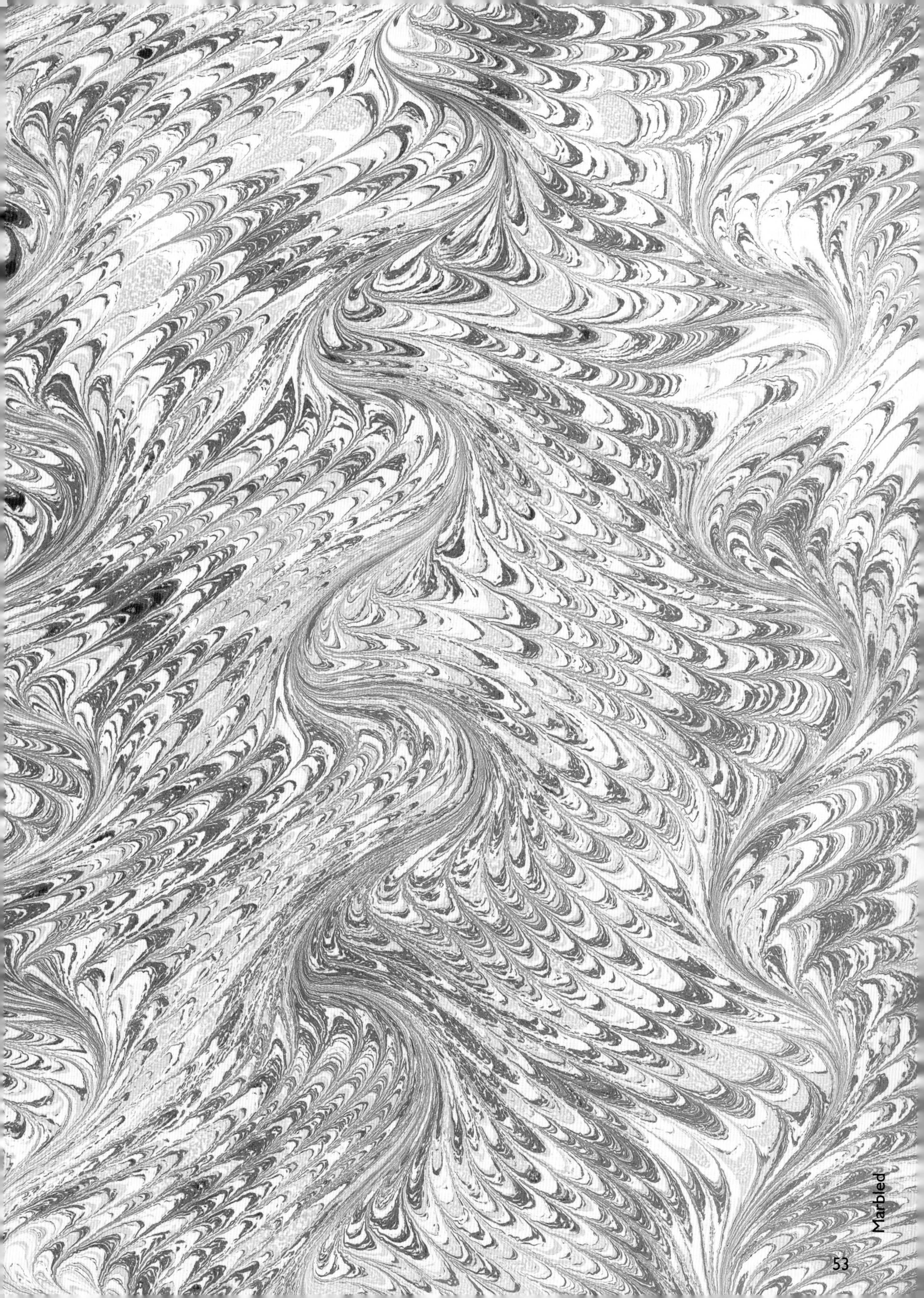

Marbled

Filter: Extrude

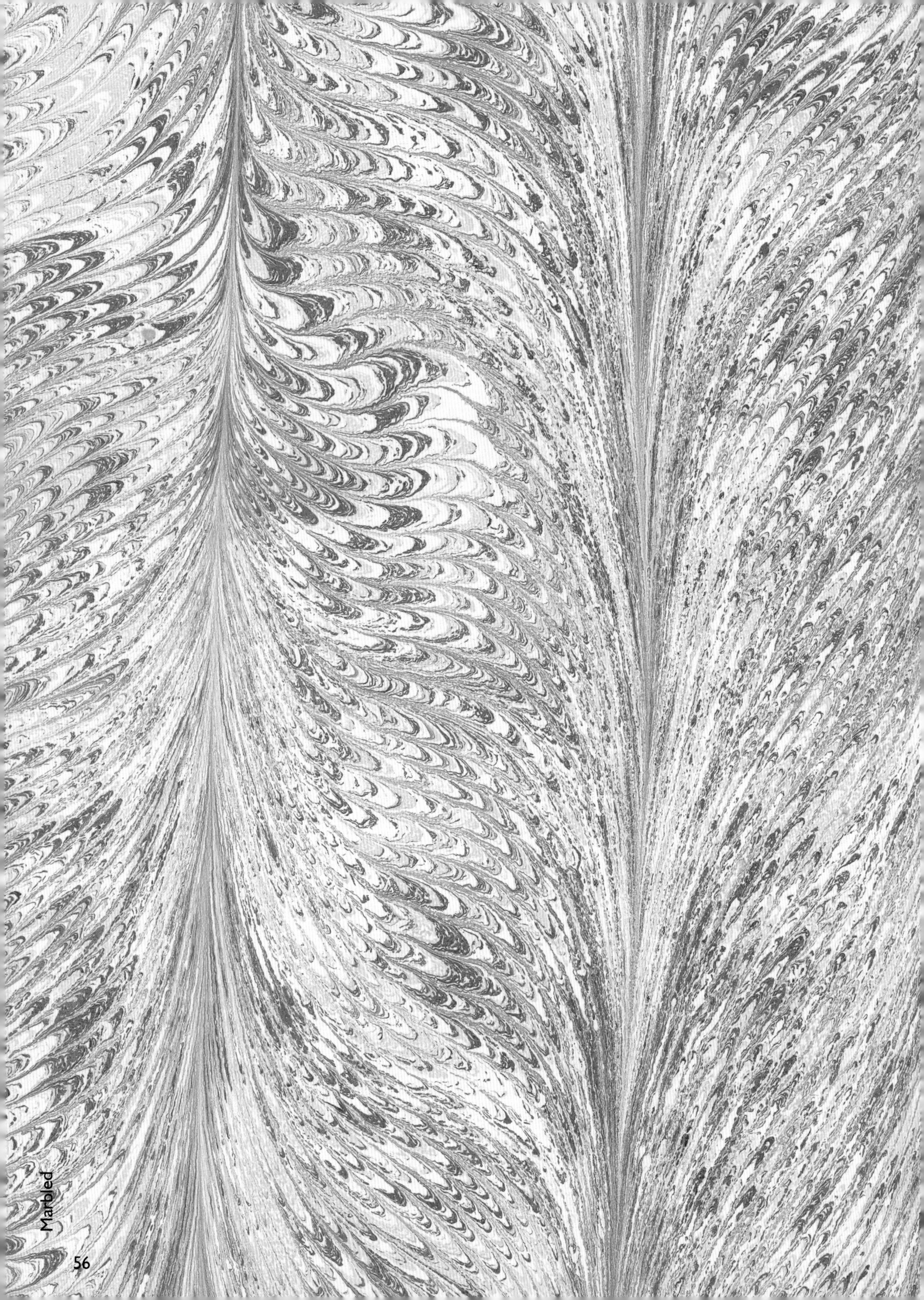

Marbled

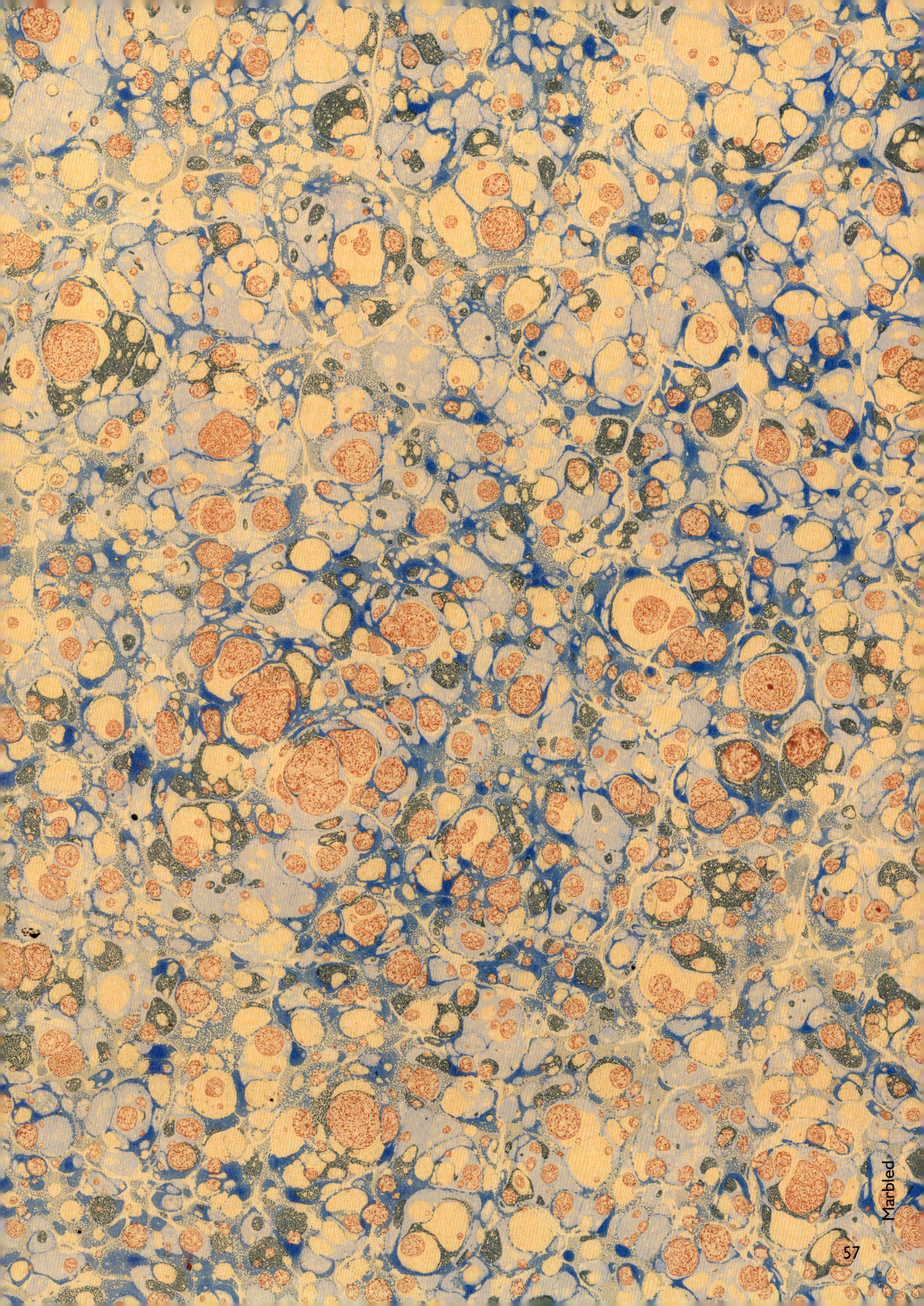

Marbled

Marbled

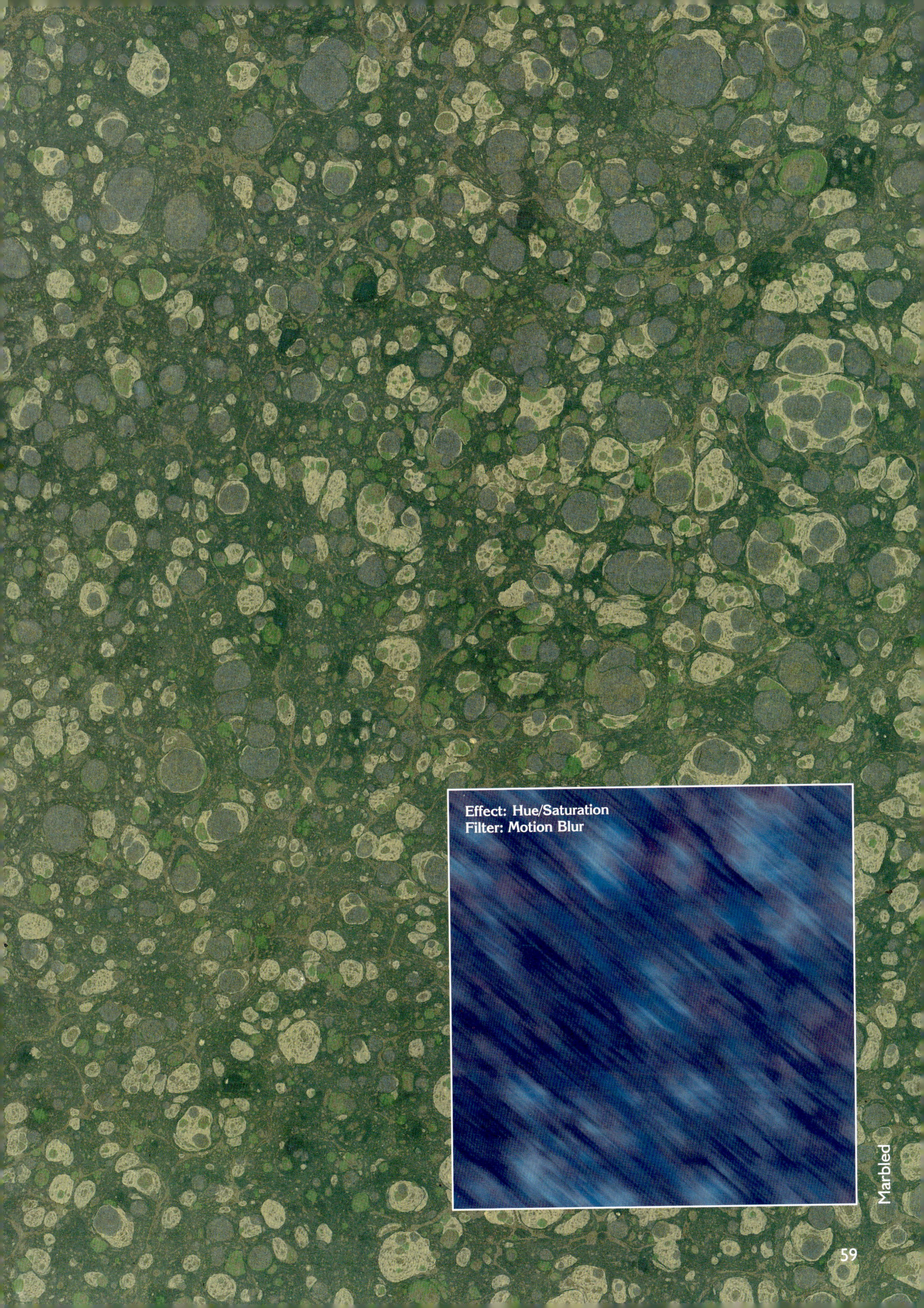

Effect: Hue/Saturation
Filter: Motion Blur

Marbled

Marbled

Marbled

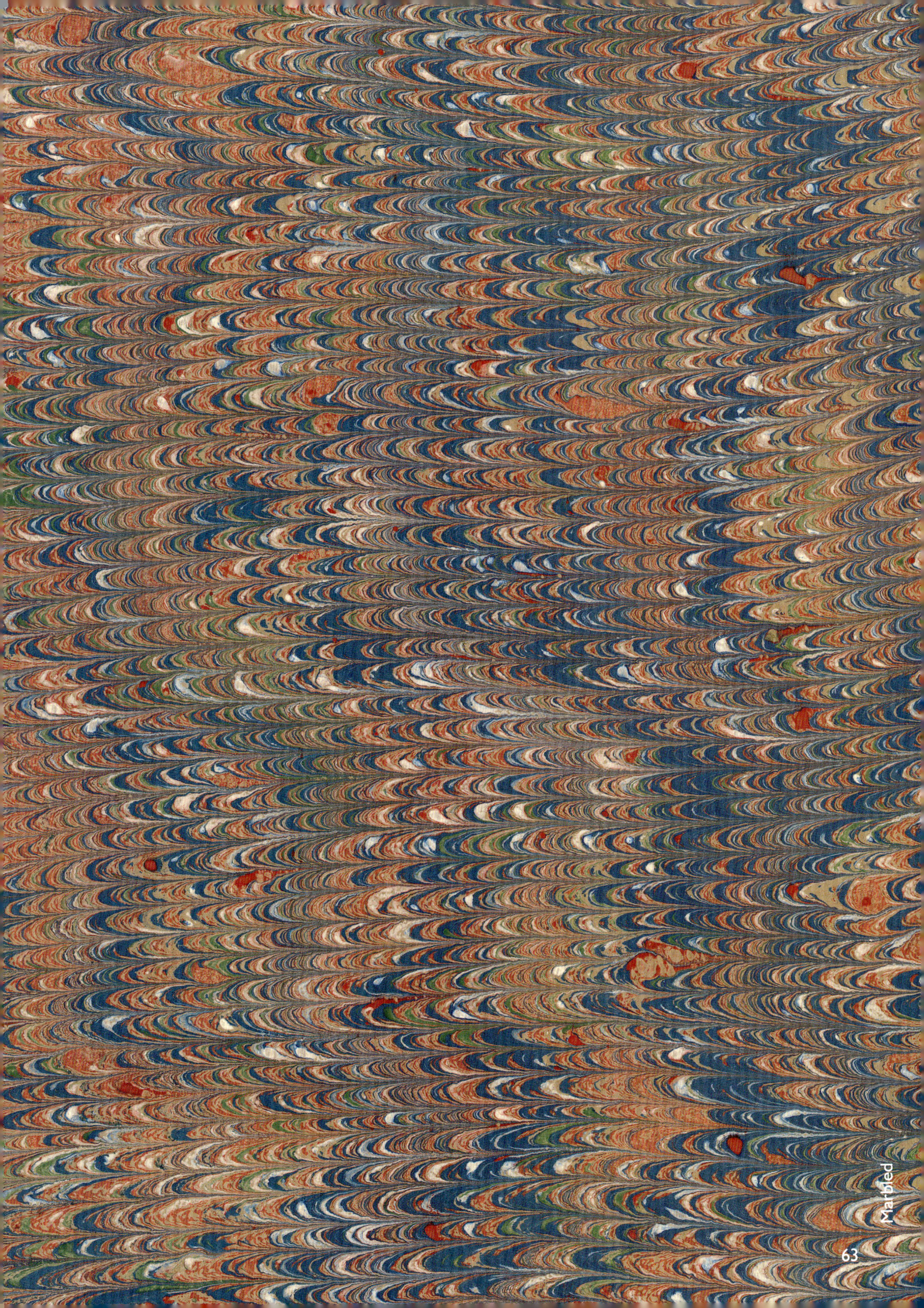

Marbled

Marbled

Filter: Crystallize

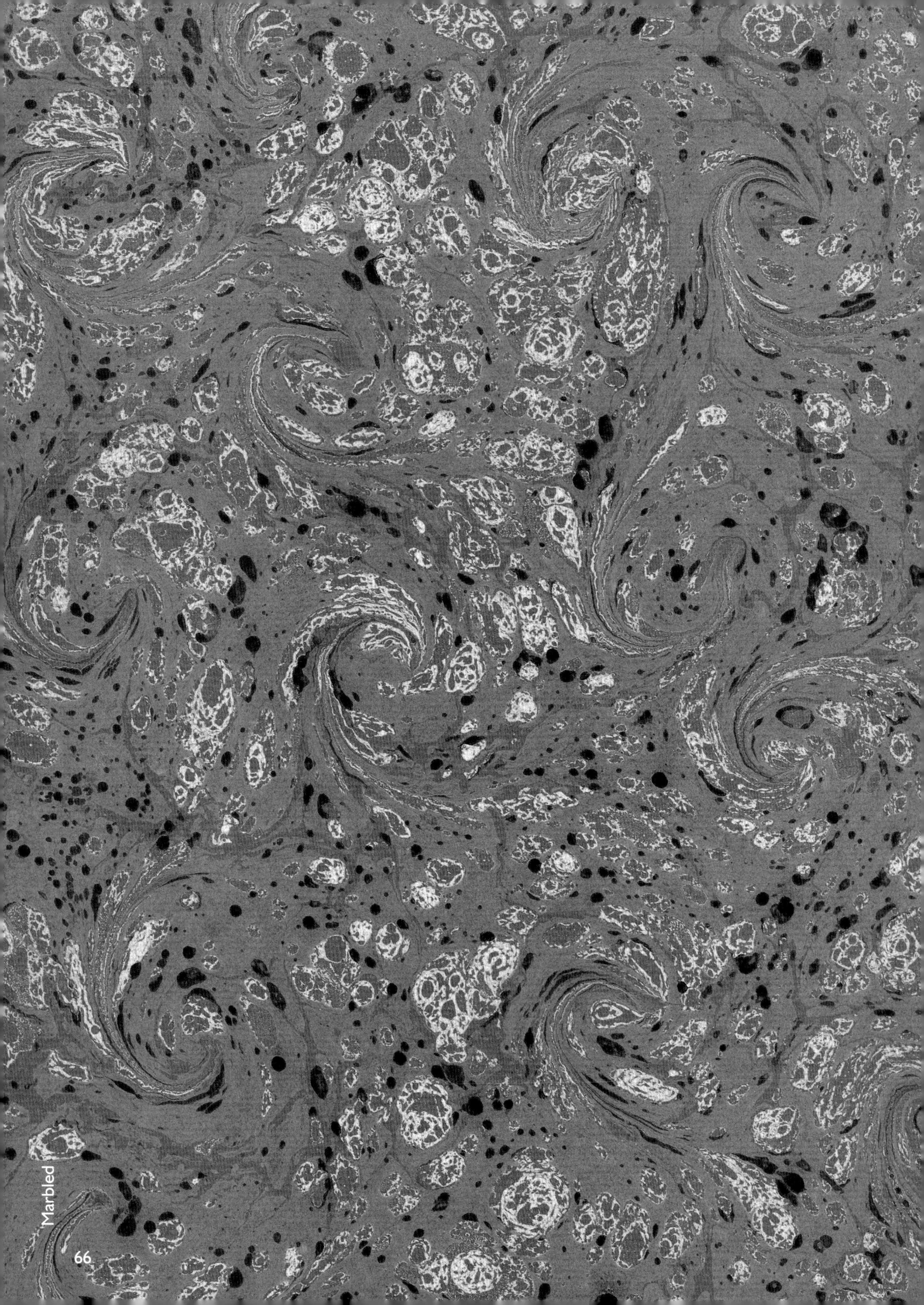

Marbled

Marbled

Marbled

Effect: Hue/Saturation
Filter: Polar Coordinates

Marbled

Marbled

Marbled

Marbled

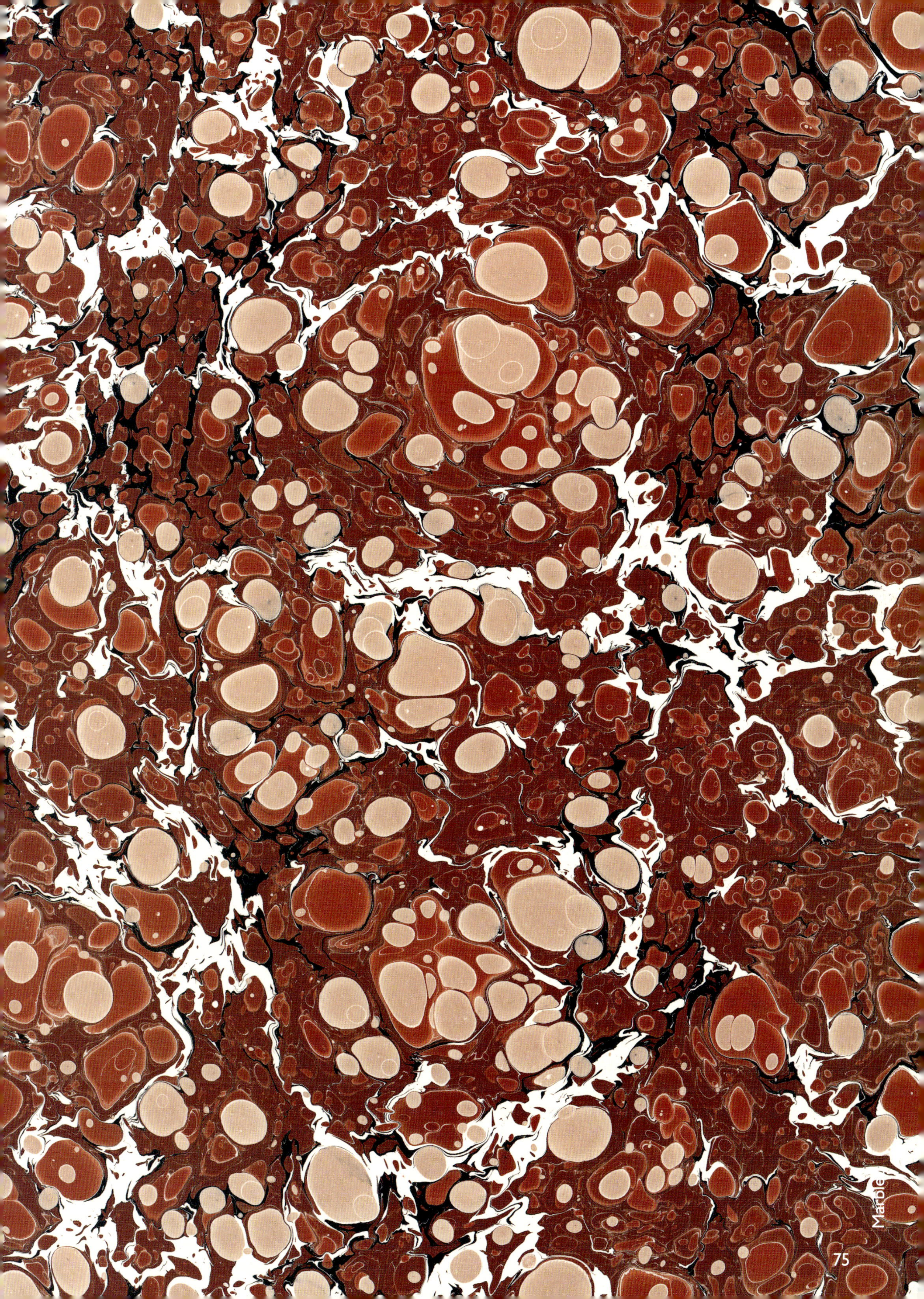

Marble

Filter: Pattern Maker

Marbled

Marbled

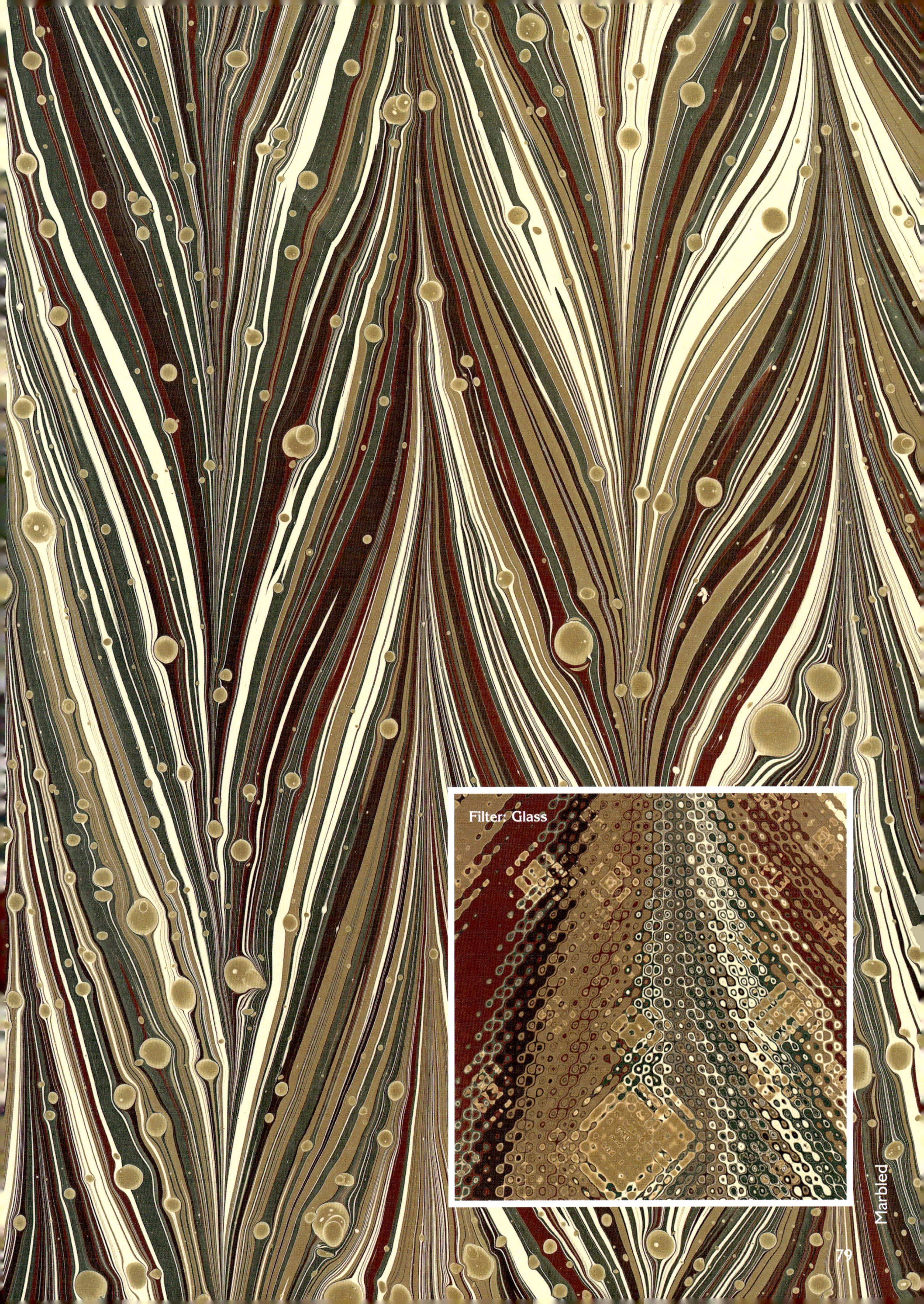

Filter: Glass

Marbled

Marbled

Effect: Hue/Saturation

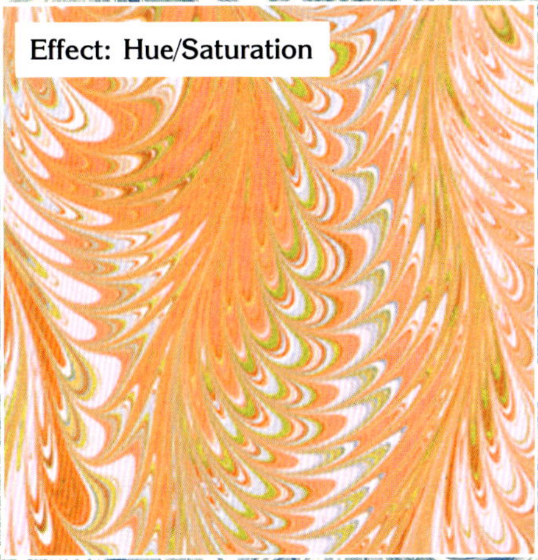

Effect: Hue/Saturation

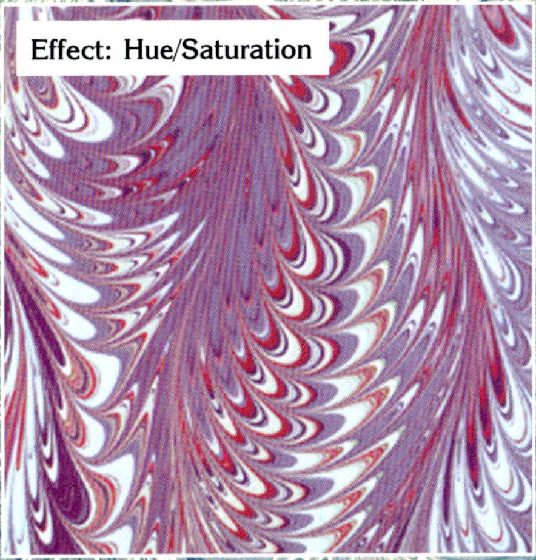

Effect: Hue/Saturation

Effect: Hue/Saturation

Marbled

Marbled
83

Marbled

Marbled

Marbled

Marbled

Filter: Diffuse Glow

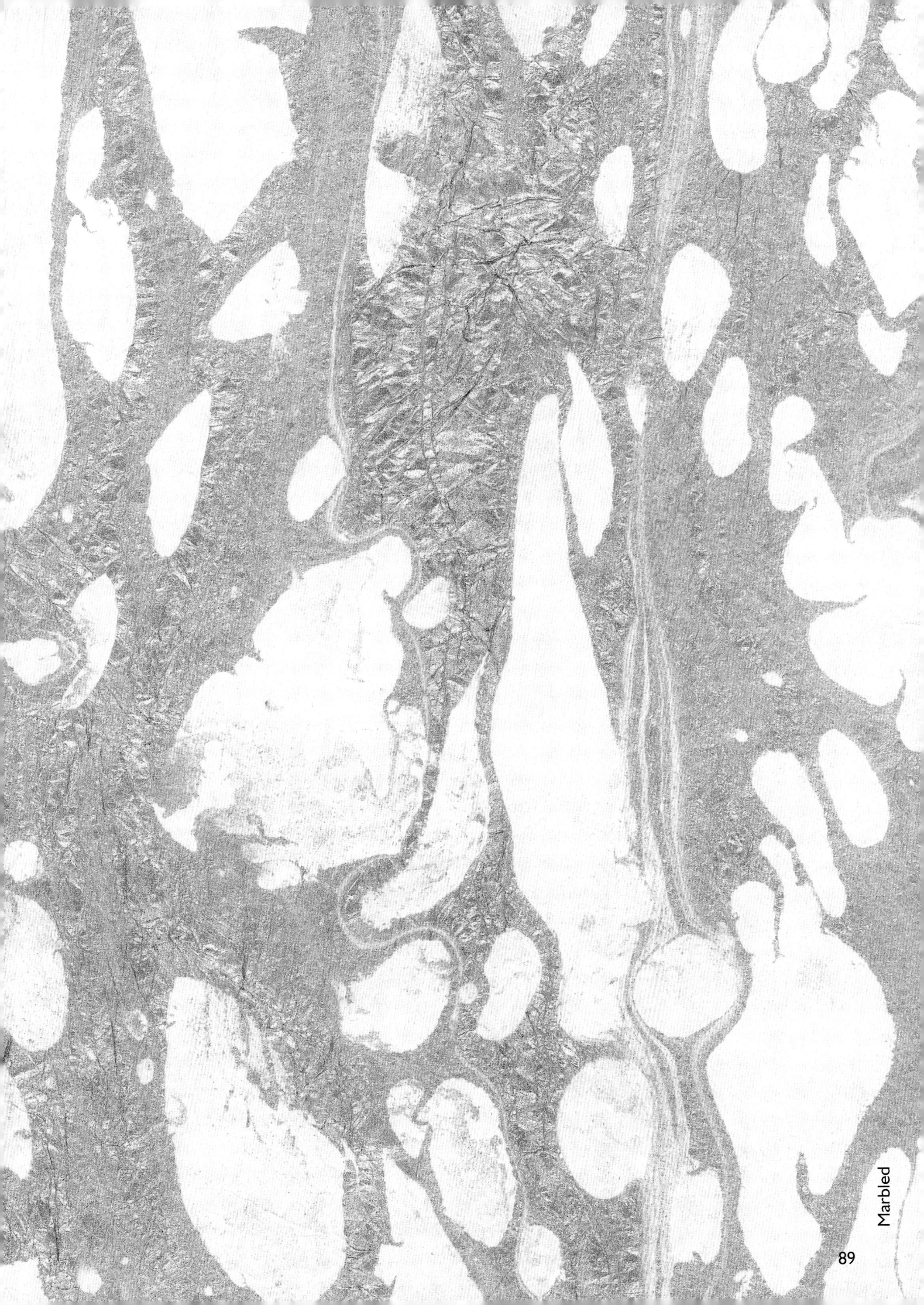

Marbled

Effect: Colorize

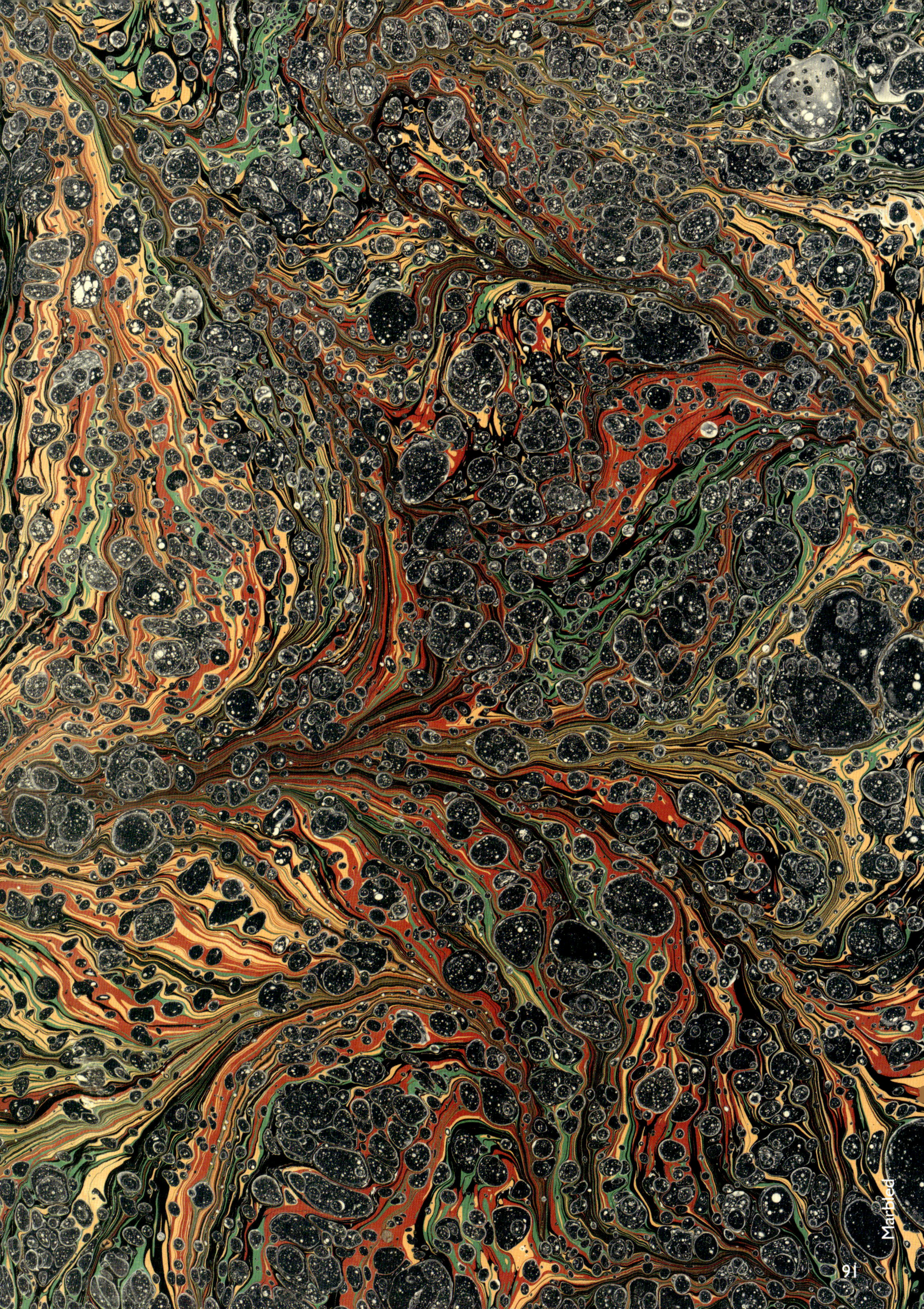

Marbled

Marbled

Marbled

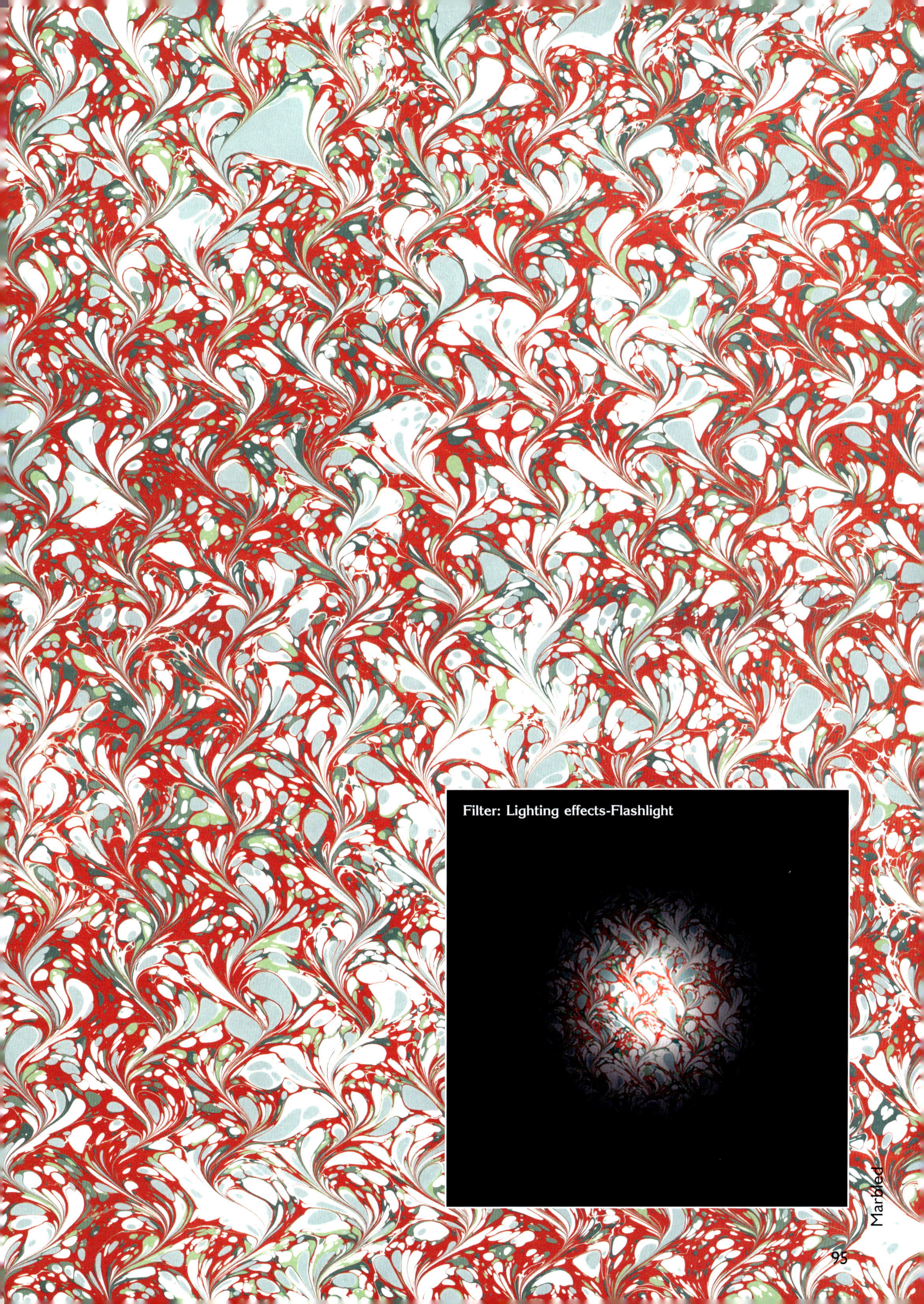

Filter: Lighting effects-Flashlight

Marbled

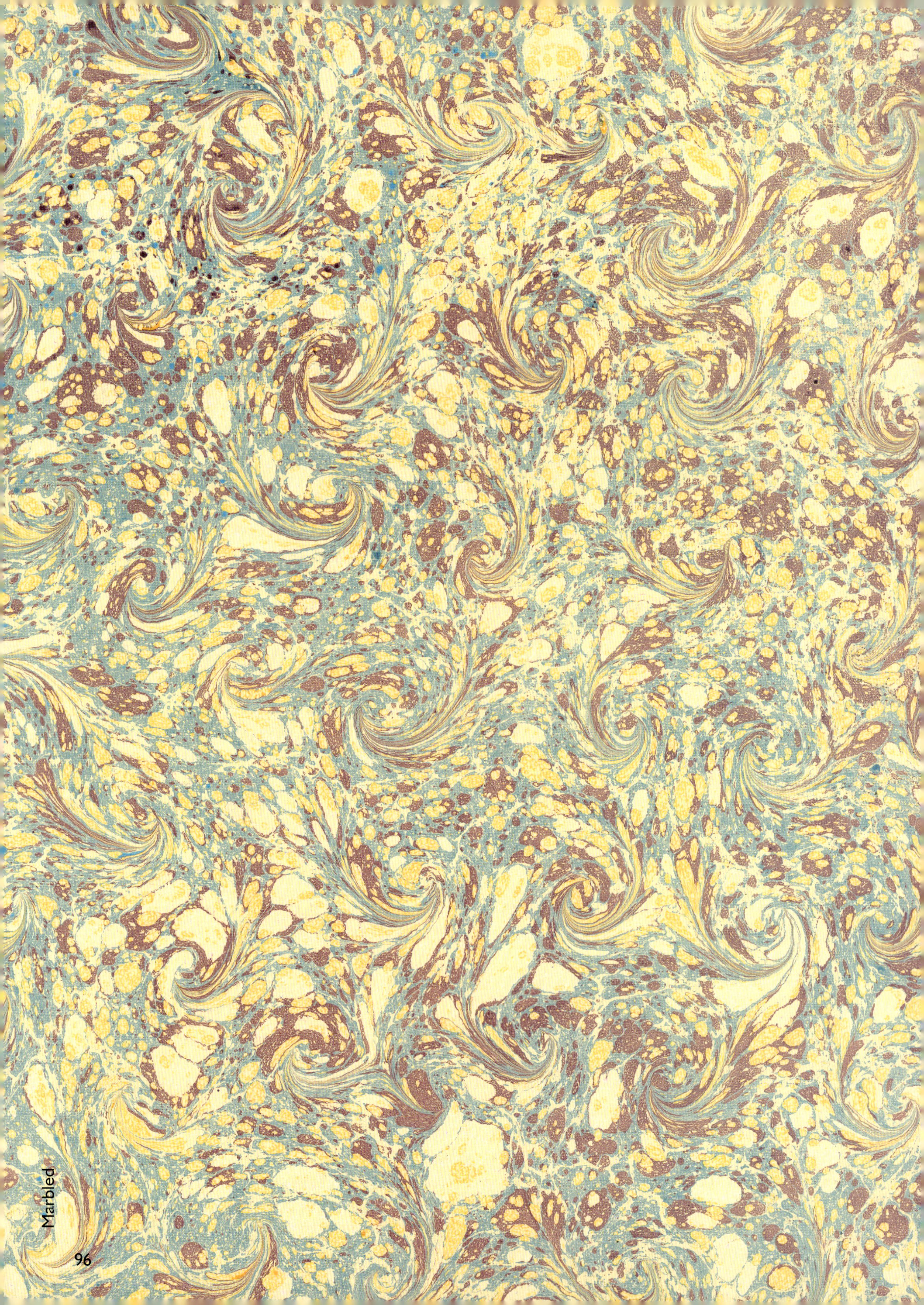

Marbled

Geometrics

99A

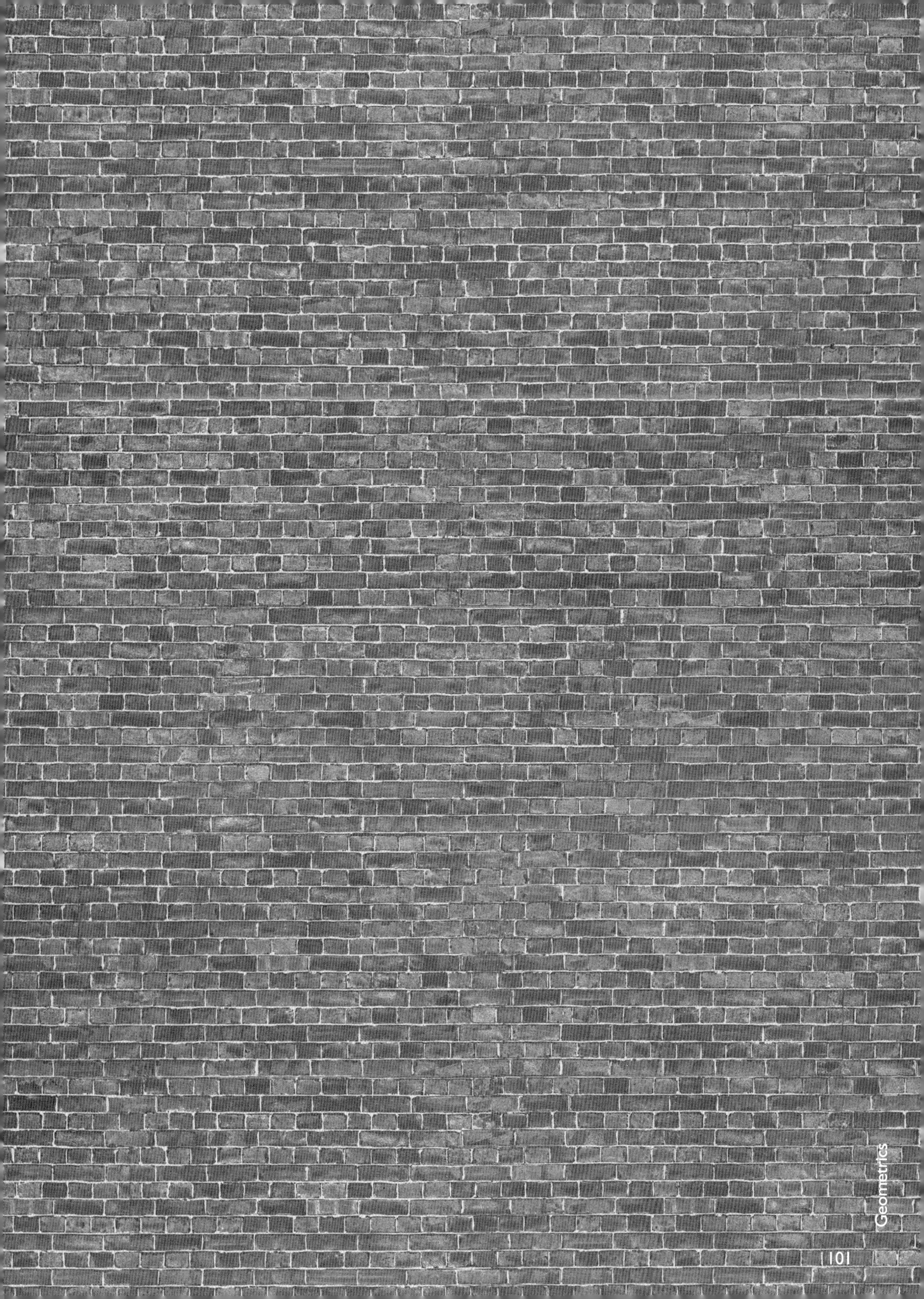

Filter: Zigzag

Miscellaneous

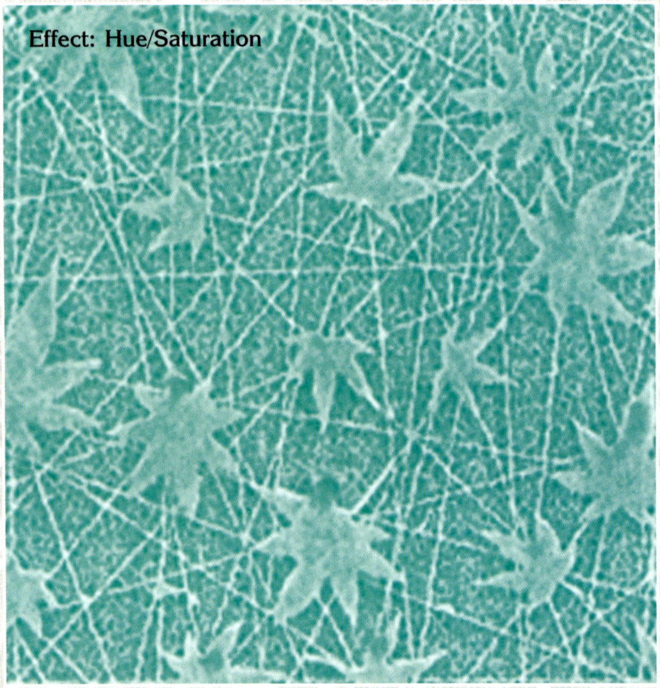

Effect: Hue/Saturation

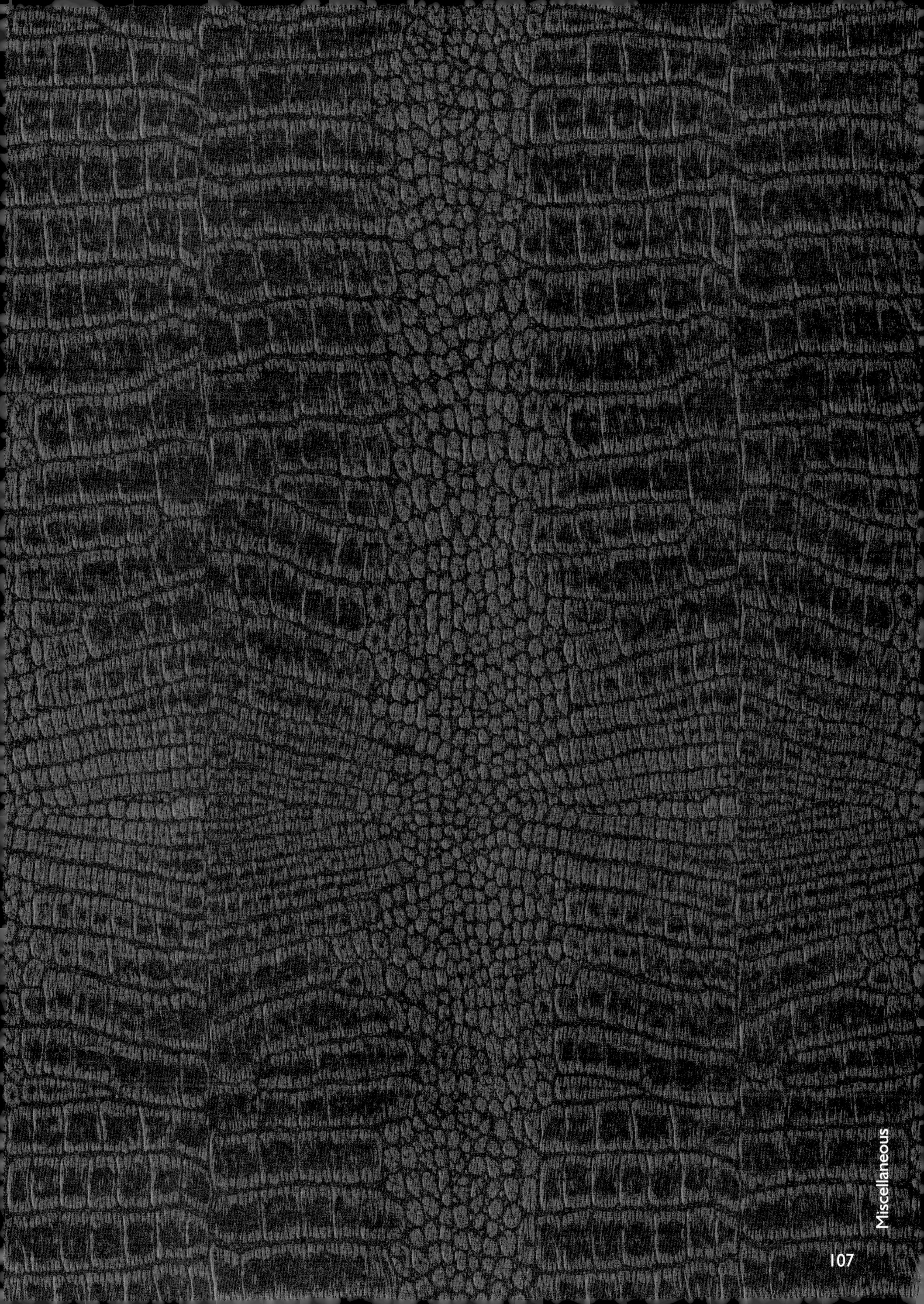

Filter: Dark brushes